Sound Waves

Published in the United States of America by Cherry Lake Publishing
Ann Arbor, Michigan
www.cherrylakepublishing.com

Reading Adviser: Marla Conn MS, Ed., Literacy specialist, Read-Ability, Inc.
Content Adviser: Brittany Burchard M.Ed., Science teacher
Book Design: Jennifer Wahi
Illustrator: Jeff Bane

Photo Credits: ©SpeedKingz/Shutterstock, 5; ©wavebreakmedia/Shutterstock, 7; ©Andrey Suslov/Shutterstock, 9; ©Brett Allen/Shutterstock, 11; ©Robert Kneschke/Shutterstock, 13; ©Vadim Sadovski/Shutterstock, 15; ©Outer Space/Shutterstock, 17; ©susana valera/Shutterstock, 19; ©antoniodiaz/Shutterstock, 21; ©adriaticfoto/Shutterstock, 23, Cover, 6, 12, 22, Jeff Bane

Library of Congress Cataloging-in-Publication Data

Names: Marsico, Katie, 1980- author.
Title: Sound waves / by Katie Marsico.
Description: Ann Arbor, Michigan : Cherry Lake Publishing, [2018] | Series:
   My world of science | Audience: K to grade 3. | Includes bibliographical
   references and index.
Identifiers: LCCN 2018003269| ISBN 9781534128941 (hardcover) | ISBN
   9781534132146 (pbk.) | ISBN 9781534130647 (pdf) | ISBN 9781534133846
   (hosted ebook)
Subjects: LCSH: Sound-waves--Juvenile literature. | Sound--Juvenile
   literature.
Classification: LCC QC243.2 .M37 2018 | DDC 534/.2--dc23
LC record available at https://lccn.loc.gov/2018003269

Printed in the United States of America
Corporate Graphics

About the author: Katie Marsico is the author of more than 200 reference books for children and young adults. She lives with her husband and six children near Chicago, Illinois.

About the illustrator: Jeff Bane and his two business partners own a studio along the American River in Folsom, California, home of the 1849 Gold Rush. When Jeff's not sketching or illustrating for clients, he's either swimming or kayaking in the river to relax.

What is sound?

How do people hear when someone sings?

Sound is a type of **energy**.

It forms when an object moves.

A moving object stirs the air around it.

Tiny pieces of air **vibrate**.

They bump into pieces next to them.

Movement spreads through the air.

It travels like a wave.

Sound waves move until they run out of energy.

How does a loud sound
change a sound wave?

Sound waves travel through **matter**. They move through gas.

They move through **liquids**.

They move through **solids**.

Sound waves don't move in some parts of **space**.

There is no matter in these areas.

Without matter, nothing vibrates.

No sound wave can form.

No sound can be heard.

Sound waves can move fast or slow.

Sound waves move slowest in gases.

They move fastest in liquids and solids.

What type of matter do
we talk through?

Sound waves travel into your ears.

Your ears and brain work together.

The brain decides what sound is being heard.

How does the shape of
our ears help us hear?

Some **scientists** study sound waves. They ask questions. They look for answers.

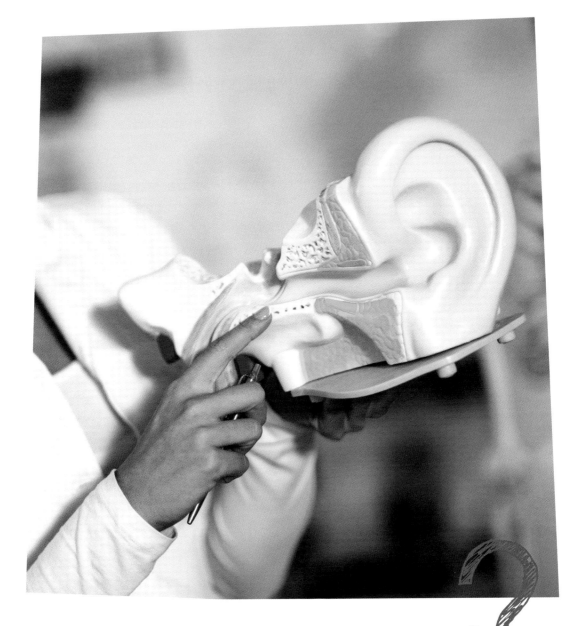

What would you like to study next?

glossary

energy (EN-ur-jee) the ability of something to do work

liquids (LIK-widz) types of matter that have a fixed size but will mold to fit whatever container they're in

matter (MAT-ur) anything that takes up space and has mass

scientists (SYE-uhn-tists) people who study nature and the world we live in

solids (SAH-lidz) types of matter that are firm and strong

space (SPAYS) the huge, dark area far beyond Earth's sky

vibrate (VYE-brayt) to move back and forth

index